UNDERSTAND CALIFORNIA SALES & USE TAX

And How to Track Them in QuickBooks

by
Tim Shortridge

Understand California Sales & Use Tax
And How to Track Them in QuickBooks

Copyright © 2018 Tim Shortridge

All rights reserved. This includes the right to reproduce any portion of this book in any form without prior written permission of the author.

For our daughter, Melanie, and our son, Richard...
We love you both past anything.

Also by
Tim Shortridge:

Understand Accounting Without Falling Asleep

Don't Cook Fish in the Company Microwave

No Place To Run

Sealing Fate

Out of Plumb

Jake

Contents

Introduction vii

1. Sales Tax vs. Use Tax..1
2. Sellers Permits 3
3. What Sales Are Subject to Sales Tax?...........................4
   What You Are Selling 5
   To Whom You Are Selling 7
   Where You Are Selling 8
4. Four Costly Mistakes to Avoid....................................13
   Not Paying Use Tax 13
   Ignoring Tax-paid Purchases.......................................14
   Overlooking Sales Tax on Handling 17
   Not Collecting Resale Certificates 19
5. Some Interesting Exceptions 21
6. Tracking Sales & Use Tax in QuickBooks.................26
   Sales Tax Charged to Customers 26
   Credits on Tax-Paid Purchases....................................32
   Use Tax 37
7. Tracking Only Use Tax 48

Introduction

The subject of sales and use taxes confuses most people, and rightly so. What is taxable? What isn't? Why? As sentient beings, we strive to comprehend the world around us. And we believe that if we study something long enough, we can understand the logic behind it. Unfortunately, the rules relating to sales and use taxes are not logical. Many of them do not seem to make any sense whatsoever.

That is because sales and use taxes are political. And rules derived from a political process of debate, special interests, and compromise are seldom logical. You cannot just figure them out. Luckily, with clear enough explanations and examples, you can come to understand them.

I did not set out in life to become an expert in California sales and use taxes. I was driven to it by the needs of my clients. Since 1992, I have been setting up accounting systems for small businesses, teaching them how to use them, and providing them with ongoing support.

Shortly after starting my practice, I took on a client who provided interior design services for the building industry. This company took the empty shells of model homes and turned them into luxurious looking residences that home buyers would want to purchase.

For a lump sum price, this company would fill these model homes with furniture, install the wallpaper, window coverings, and flooring, and bring in enough knickknacks to make each place look as if someone lived there.

When I took on this client, I had no idea their business model was a sales tax nightmare. For years, I studied the rules of the California State Board of Equalization just to keep this client out of trouble. By 2010, I was so well versed in California's rules for sales and use taxes that I developed and taught a sales tax workshop for SCORE, a resource partner of the U.S. Small Business Administration.

This book is derived from the materials of that workshop.

I hope you find it helpful.

Bureaucratic Change on July 1, 2017

Beginning on July 1, 2017, the sales and use tax duties previously performed by the California State Board of Equalization (BOE) were transferred to the newly created California Department of Tax and Fee Administration (CDTFA).

All of the rules, regulations, and forms remained the same. Probably the biggest change was the new website address of *www.cdtfa.ca.gov*, although during the transition the new website just transferred everyone to the old BOE website.

A Quick Note on Learning

In his book, *The 7 Habits of Highly Effective People*, Stephen R. Covey describes a way to significantly improve a person's understanding of anything they study. Rather than study for the purpose of learning, you should study for the purpose of teaching someone else.

By studying with the intention of teaching someone else, you change how you view the material you are studying, and that paradigm shift greatly improves your ability to understand.

I have found this technique quite effective, and I recommend you do the following:

1. Think of someone you know who could benefit from a better understanding of sales and use tax.
2. Contact them now, before you proceed, and set up a time to meet within the next few weeks.
3. While you study this book, take notes on how *you* will teach this material to them.
4. Keep your appointment and teach them these basics.

If you do this, both of you will benefit.

A Note on QuickBooks Versions

This book is based on the 2018 version of QuickBooks Desktop Pro. If you use a different version, then the specific steps I list may be slightly different. However, the general concepts of tracking and reporting will be the same.

This is also true for other accounting software. The basic concepts apply even if their implementation is different.

In addition, I chose not to use account numbers in the Chart of Accounts. If you do use account numbers, assign whatever numbers work within your numbering system.

Understand California Sales & Use Tax

And How to Track Them
in QuickBooks

Chapter 1

Sales Tax vs. Use Tax

What is the difference between sales taxes and use taxes?

Short Answer: Not much.

They both have the same tax rates. They both apply to the same goods that are sold. They both are paid by the buyer. They both are collected by the State of California. Practically everything about them is identical except for one thing.

Sales Taxes are paid by the buyer *to the seller* at the time the sale takes place. The seller then pays them to the State of California.
Use Taxes are paid by the buyer *directly to the State of California.*

For example, when you buy a used car from a dealer, the car dealer charges you sales tax as part of your purchase. The car dealer will send those sales taxes to the State of California when they file their sales tax return with the California Department of Tax and Fee Administration (CDTFA).

However, what happens when you buy a car from a private party? They do not charge you sales tax. But when you go to the Department of Motor Vehicles (DMV) to register the car, the DMV will assess you use tax on your purchase as part of the registration process. You are paying the use tax directly to the State of California.

The use tax you pay the DMV is identical to the sales tax you would pay to a dealer, except that you paid it directly to the State of California.

Here is a business example. When your business buys a computer from a local store, that store will charge you sales tax as part of the purchase and send it to the CDTFA.

However, if your business buys the same computer online from a vendor outside of California, that vendor might not charge you sales tax on the computer. Your business would then be required to pay use tax on your purchase of that computer directly to the State of California, either to the CDTFA on your sales tax return (or a separate use tax return) or to the Franchise Tax Board on your income tax return.

So, if these two taxes are practically identical, why not just call them both sales tax? Why have two different names that might create confusion? Here is one of the many places where logic breaks down and politics take over.

There does not appear to be any logical reason to call them by different names. It is just the way it is.

Kind of like when your parents would tell you to do something and you would ask, "Why?" And they would answer with, "Because I said so."

In this case, it is because the State of California says so.

Chapter 2

Sellers Permits

The California Department of Tax and Fee Administration (CDTFA) issues sellers permits to businesses authorizing them to collect sales tax on behalf of the State of California. You are required to have a sellers permit if you fit this definition:

> *"Anyone engaged in business in California who sells (or leases) tangible personal property that would be subject to sales tax if sold at retail."*

Clear as mud, right? We will spend the next chapter clarifying exactly what that sentence means. In the meantime, perhaps this will help.

Short Answer: Anyone selling (or leasing) things subject to sales tax.

If you are making sales that are subject to sales tax, then you are required to have a sellers permit. And it is important to remember that if this applies to you, you are required to have a seller permit *before* you begin selling in California.

You might be thinking, "Okay. Then what sales are subject to sales tax?" Thank you for asking.

Chapter 3

What Sales Are Subject to Sales Tax?

Short Answer: Anything the California Department of Tax and Fee Administration says is subject to sales tax.

Back to Mom and Dad saying, "Because I said so."

However, *in general*, there are three criteria that determine whether or not a sale is taxable, and they are:

1. What you are selling.
2. To whom you are selling.
3. Where you are selling.

All three criteria must be present for a sale to be taxable. In other words, you must be selling *something* that is taxable to *a buyer* who is taxable in a *location* that is taxable.

If any one of these three criteria are absent, then the sale is not taxable.

Before we look at each criterion closer, notice I said there are three criteria *in general*. I said that because rules derived from a political process always have exceptions, and this is especially true for sales and use taxes. Becoming familiar with the exceptions in your industry will be your greatest challenge and listing all the exceptions for every industry is well beyond the scope of this discussion.

The CDTFA has booklets for every industry that list all the exceptions. These booklets can be downloaded for free on their website at ***www.cdtfa.ca.gov***.

I recommend you download the booklet for your industry and study it. As I mentioned in the Introduction, sales and use taxes are not something you can just figure out because they are not logical. All you can do is familiarize yourself with the rules. My goal with this book is to make your further research easier. However, you will still need to do it.

And please do not base how you do your sales taxes on how other business owners you may know do their sales taxes. I have met many business owners who thought, "If that is how my competitor is doing it, then it must be right." And most of these business owners were mistaken.

Many companies, including many large companies, have been required to change how they charge sales taxes because they were doing it wrong, and they lost their battle with the CDTFA. Battling the CDTFA is not something I recommend you attempt to do.

What You Are Selling

Remember who the California Department of Tax and Fee Administration said needed a sellers permit:

> *"Anyone engaged in business in California who sells (or leases) **tangible personal property** that would be subject to sales tax if sold at retail."*

Let's take a closer look at the meaning of *tangible personal property*.

Tangible means you can touch it. So, in general, if you cannot touch what you are selling, then it is not taxable. For example, if you sell services such as consulting, accounting, or car washing, your services cannot be touched and are therefore not taxable.

Furniture, equipment, and office supplies can be touched. Therefore, they are taxable.

If you sell a computer program on a CD, then you would charge sales tax on the sale of the program because you can touch the CD. However, if you sell that same program via download, then you do not have to charge sales tax because you cannot touch the downloaded program.

Remember, though, there are exceptions to this rule as there are exceptions to all the sales tax rules. Some things you can touch are not taxable (e.g. most groceries), and some things you cannot touch are taxable (e.g. fabrication labor).

Personal property means you can move it around. If you cannot move what you are selling, then, in general, it is not taxable. For example, real estate is not taxable. If you sell land, you do not charge sales tax. If you sell a house that is built on land, then you do not charge sales tax.

However, if you sell a mobile home, then you do charge sales tax on the sale because a mobile home can be moved.

Of course, a house could be moved if you disconnected it from the land and put it on a trailer. So, if you sell a house on a trailer, then you would charge sales tax. But as long as the house is affixed to the ground, you do not have to charge sales tax on its sale.

Therefore, ***tangible personal property*** is anything you can touch and move around. Most tangible personal property is taxable. We will discuss some exceptions in a later chapter.

To Whom You Are Selling

Most *end users* are taxable. An end user is the person who will be using the thing you are selling. In general, when you sell something to a person who is planning on using that thing, that buyer is taxable.

For example, if you sell computers (tangible personal property) to an accounting firm that needs them to do accounting work for their clients, then that accounting firm is taxable because they are going to be *using* the computers.

However, if you sell the same computers to a computer consulting firm that will be selling the computers to their clients, then that computer consulting firm is not the end user. They are *resellers* of the computers, and you would not charge them sales tax (so long as you had a resale certificate on file for them - see full explanation on page 19).

There are two major exceptions to the end user rule:

1. The Federal Government.
2. Indian Reservations.

If you sell those same computers to either the Federal Government or an Indian Reservation who is planning to use them, that sale is not taxable.

Why? Because the State of California says so.

Where You Are Selling

Where you are selling depends on where you deliver your product to your customer.

For example, if your customer stops by your store, buys something, and walks out the door with it. Then that sale takes place in your store.

If a customer orders something on your website, or on the phone, and you ship it to them through the post office, then that sale takes place at the address where you shipped it.

The good news is, you are only required to collect sales taxes on orders that take place in a location where you have *nexus*. Nexus means you have a business presence there.

If you have any of the following in a California location, then you have nexus there and are required to charge the sales tax rate of that location:

1. Physical presence, whether owning or leasing:
   - a store or an office.
   - a warehouse or storage facility.
   - a computer server.
2. Rental or lease income from tangible personal property in that location.

What Sales are Subject to Sales Tax?

3. An employee, independent contractor, or agent operating on your behalf:
   - selling.
   - delivering.
   - installing.
   - assembling.
   - establishing or maintaining a market.
4. Inventory being manufactured or stored.

If you have any of these four things anywhere inside the State of California, then you have nexus in each place they are located, and you are required to collect the applicable sales tax on sales you make in each of those locations.

Once you know you are required to charge your customers sales tax, it is important that you collect the correct amount that applies for the location of the sale.

California sales tax rates have three components:

1. State Sales Tax.
2. County Sales Tax.
3. City Sales Tax.

Luckily, all three sales taxes are filed and paid to the same entity, the CDTFA.

For example, as of this writing, the State sales tax rate is 7.25%, the County of San Diego sales tax rate is .5%, and the city of La Mesa sales tax rate is .75%.

If you have a store in the city of La Mesa, then you have nexus in California, San Diego County, and the city of La Mesa. Therefore, you would charge customers shopping in your store a total sales tax rate of 8.5% (7.25% + .5% + .75%), and you would remit the entire amount to the CDTFA on your sales tax return.

On the other hand, if your store is located in Simi Valley, then you have nexus in California, Ventura County, and the city of Simi Valley. However, as of this writing, you only have to charge 7.25% because both the county of Ventura and the city of Simi Valley have sales tax rates of 0%.

Let's say your store is located in the city of La Mesa which has a sales tax rate of 8.5%. A customer from San Francisco places a taxable order on your website and requests that you ship it to them. Let's also say that you do not have nexus in either the county or city of San Francisco. In this case, you are only required to charge your customer the California rate of 7.25%. Even though you do not have nexus in San Francisco, you still have nexus in California.

If that same on-line customer is from Las Vegas, and you do not have nexus in Nevada, then you would not have to charge them any sales tax.

At this point, you might be thinking that this is way too complicated to deal with. How on earth are you going to keep track of it all? Later on, I will explain how to keep track of all this in QuickBooks. Even if you do not use QuickBooks, the overall tracking strategies I describe can be applied with any accounting software even if the specific steps will be slightly different.

You may have another option. Many smaller companies choose not to deal with all the different sales tax rates. If your local sales tax rate is higher than any of the other locations where you have nexus, then the CDTFA is fine with you charging your local (and higher) tax rate to all your customers. That is, of course, so long as you send all the sales tax you collect to the CDTFA.

Of course, this simple solution will not work if your clients object. You might even have a client request that you collect the correct sales tax for their location, even if you do not have nexus, just so they will not have to be bothered with paying use tax on their purchase.

These are all business decisions you need to make, and you must decide what is best for your business.

Sales tax rates fluctuate regularly. And it is important that you charge the current rates. After you register for a sellers permit with the CDTFA, they will email you updates whenever the rates change. If you keep your rates updated in QuickBooks (or whatever accounting software you use), then you should not have any problem collecting the correct amount.

At any time, you can access and download the latest sales tax rates on the CDTFA's website at ***www.cdtfa.ca.gov***.

In Summary

For a sale to be taxable, you must be doing all three of the following:

1. Selling tangible personal property that is not excluded for some reason (e.g. groceries).
2. Selling to a taxable end user, not a reseller, Federal Government, or Indian Reservation.
3. Selling in a location where you have nexus.

The tax rate you are required to charge may include the tax rates for the State, County, or City, depending on your nexus status in the location where the sale takes place.

Chapter 4
Four Costly Mistakes to Avoid

Over the years, I have seen the following four mistakes made countless times by business owners and their bookkeepers. These mistakes have cost these business owners many hours of worry and tens of thousands of dollars.

This is your opportunity to learn from the mistakes of these other businesses. Do not make the same mistakes, and save yourself from the stress and financial risk.

In my experience, the California Department of Tax and Fee Administration (CDTFA) is not an agency with which you want to do battle. They are not as nice as the Internal Revenue Service (IRS). The IRS knows that they are asking you to give them *your* money to pay your taxes. But the CDTFA is demanding that you give them *their* money that you are responsible for collecting on their behalf. It was never your money in the first place.

Mistake #1
Not Paying Use Tax

The most common mistake is buying something taxable and not paying use tax on it. If an out-of-state vendor does not charge you sales tax, you are still responsible for paying your local sales tax on your purchase to the State of California in the form of use taxes.

In the event of a sales tax audit, one of the first things the CDTFA will want to see are the purchase documents for all your furniture, computers, and equipment. They will be looking for any out-of-state purchases where the vendor did not charge you sales tax. They will also look for any private-party purchases that did not include sales tax.

The CDTFA might even ask to see all your Amazon purchases since many of Amazon's third-party vendors continue to not charge California sales taxes.

I had one client who purchased over $50,000 in restaurant equipment from out-of-state and private-party sellers. Ignoring my suggestion, he refused to pay the use taxes. During an audit some years later, the CDTFA accused him of intentionally trying to avoid paying his taxes. The CDTFA then expanded the scope of their audit beyond the typical three years, and eventually billed this client over $15,000 in back taxes, interest, and penalties. The owner had to take out a second mortgage on his home just to stay in business.

Do not make the same mistake. It is not worth the risk.

You can pay use taxes by adding them to your sales tax return, adding them to your state income tax return, or paying them online as a one-time payment.

Mistake #2
Ignoring Tax-paid Purchases

Unlike Mistake #1, Mistake #2 will not get you in trouble with the CDTFA. In fact, the CDTFA never complains if you pay them more money than you owe them.

Four Costly Mistakes to Avoid

When you buy something taxable that you plan to resell, you do not have to pay sales tax on it. In this case, you are a reseller, so your vendor is not required to charge you sales tax.

Sometimes, however, your vendor charges you sales tax anyway. This is called a ***Tax-paid Purchase, Resold Prior to Use***. When this happens, you are entitled to deduct the sales tax you paid your vendor from what you owe the CDTFA.

If you do not deduct it, then the CDTFA will have been paid twice; once by your vendor charging you sales tax, and again by you charging your customer sales tax. Therefore, the CDTFA entitles you to deduct what you paid your vendor from the amount you collect from your customer.

Over time, double paying the CDTFA can add up to a lot of money.

The design company I mentioned in the Introduction saved thousands of dollars annually by tracking and reporting all tax-paid purchases. During their model home installations, the design staff would go crazy trying to get everything delivered and installed in a few short days. They would spend thousands of dollars in local retail stores for additional supplies and knickknacks to ensure each model home looked like someone lived there. Since they were charging the builder sales tax on all that tangible personal property, they tracked the sales taxes paid on each receipt to ensure they deducted everything possible on their sales tax returns.

I will explain how to do this in the later chapter on tracking sales tax in QuickBooks.

The CDTFA audited that client repeatedly due to the complexity of their returns, and they never had a problem with the deductions they made for the tax-paid purchases.

Another example are flooring retailers. The flooring retailers I work with typically include installation in the lump sum price of the carpet, tile, or vinyl flooring they sell.

When flooring is installed, it becomes affixed to the real estate and is no longer considered tangible personal property. Therefore, the CDTFA says that the flooring company is selling real estate and should not charge their customers sales tax. However, since they are not charging their customers sales tax, then they are the end users of the flooring materials and must pay sales tax on their purchases of the flooring.

Basically, the CDTFA is saying that someone has to pay the sales tax, and if it is not the flooring company's customers, them it has to be the flooring company.

My flooring company clients do not charge their customers sales tax on installed flooring, and they have all their flooring vendors charge them sales tax on their purchases.

Occasionally, however, some customers buy the flooring without the installation. Uninstalled flooring is definitely tangible personal property and subject to sales tax. So, my clients charge those customers sales tax. They also track the sales tax on the purchases for these *Material Only* sales and deduct them on their sales tax returns.

Again, these deductions total thousands of dollars each year, far more than the cost of accounting for them.

If you track these tax-paid purchases, you could save yourself a significant amount of money.

Mistake #3
Overlooking Sales Tax on Handling

If you charge shipping and handling, the CDTFA says the handling portion is taxable. And handling is defined as any amount you charge for shipping that exceeds your actual cost of shipping, whether you call it handling or not.

For example, let's say you add shipping of $8.95 to all your online orders because most of them cost you $8.95 to ship. However, some of your orders only cost you $6.50 to ship. Then you are required to charge sales tax on the $2.45 difference on each order that only costs $6.50 to ship.

Is this unbelievable? Absolutely. Do you really have to do it? The CDTFA says you do. I see five choices here.

Your first and easiest choice is to ignore the rule. In the event of an audit, the CDTFA will estimate all the sales taxes you did not collect for at least the prior three years, and possibly the prior eight years. They will then bill you for all those taxes, plus penalties, plus interest. The sales tax on each sale may only be pennies, but if you are doing hundreds of sales each month over a period of three to eight years, that tax bill could total many thousands of dollars.

I do not recommend you ignore this rule.

Your second choice would be to charge your customers only for your exact shipping costs and never include handling. I do not recommend this choice either as you are refusing to charge your customers dollars in order to save yourself pennies. That is not good business.

Your third choice is to separate the shipping and handling charges on each sale. If you do this, then you can charge sales tax on the handling. If your customers would be okay with seeing how much you charge them for handling, then this could work. In my experience, however, customers do not mind paying a combined amount for shipping and handling, but when it is separated they frequently object.

Your fourth choice is to create an elaborate accounting system that can track the difference between your shipping cost and what you charge your customers for shipping and handling. Unfortunately, the cost of creating and maintaining an accounting system for this purpose could easily exceed any benefit you could derive from it.

Your fifth and easiest choice that will keep you out of trouble with the CDTFA is to charge sales tax on the entire amount of shipping and handling. As long as the amount you charge for shipping and handling is small, then your customers will probably never notice that you are overcharging them for the sales tax on your cost of shipping, and of course the CDTFA is okay with you doing that so long as you send all the taxes you collect to them.

Some people feel like handling should not be taxable because it is the amount you are charging your customer for the labor of shipping a product to them, and labor is not taxable. The CDTFA does not look at handling as the amount you are charging for the labor of shipping. They consider it the amount you are charging for the box, packing material, strapping tape, label and anything else you use to ship the product. In other words, you are selling your customer all your packaging and must charge them sales tax on this tangible personal property.

Since you are selling this packaging to your customer, and you are required to charge them sales tax, then you do not have to pay the sales tax when you buy those shipping supplies. If you do pay your vendor sales tax on shipping supplies, be sure to keep track of those tax-paid purchases so you can deduct it from what you owe the CDTFA.

Mistake #4
Not Collecting Resale Certificates

You are not required to charge any customer sales tax if that customer is buying your products for the purpose of reselling them to their own customers.

However, you are required to collect from each of those resale customers a *Resale Certificate* before you stop charging them sales tax.

A Resale Certificate is a statement from your customer that says they hold a valid sellers permit and are buying your products for the purpose of resale.

The CDTFA has a blank form you can download on their website at ***www.cdtfa.ca.gov***. Download it and have every one of your resale customers complete and sign it *before* you stop charging them sales tax.

A common mistake I have seen is companies who think a copy of their customer's sellers permit is good enough to satisfy the CDTFA. It is not.

A Resale Certificate is *not* a copy of your customer's sellers permit. It is a statement, signed by your customer, that says they are buying your products for the purpose of resale. That statement is what releases you from the responsibility of charging them sales tax.

Just because your client has a sellers permit does not mean they are buying your products for the purpose of resale. They could be buying your products to use in their business. How do you know what they are doing with the products you sell them?

In the event of a sales tax audit, the CDTFA will ask to see your resale certificates. If you do not have them, the CDTFA can charge you for all the sales tax you did not collect from your resale customers going back three years. Imagine how much that could be.

Do not take the risk. Do it right and stay out of trouble.

Chapter 5

Some Interesting Exceptions

Some of the exceptions to the sales tax rules are real head scratchers. Let me share with you some odd ones. This is certainly not a complete list, and you should download the booklet on your industry at *www.cdtfa.ca.gov* so you can familiarize yourself with all the exceptions that could impact your business.

Food has more exceptions than most other categories.

Groceries

In general, groceries are not subject to sales tax even though they are tangible personal property. When you buy food, grocery stores do not tax most of your purchases. There are some interesting exceptions to this exception.

Most snacks are taxable. This includes chips and candy.

Hot food is taxable. If you buy a cooked rotisserie chicken that is hot, it is taxable. If you buy a hot sandwich, it is taxable. If you buy the same chicken or sandwich, but they are not hot, then they are not taxable.

Beverages

Bottled drinks are not taxable, unless they are carbonated. Carbonated drinks are taxable. Commonly referred to as the *Bubble Tax*.

Restaurants

Everything consumed in a restaurant is taxable.

Therefore, they ask, "Is this order for-here or to-go?"

Not all items taken out of a restaurant are taxable. If an item is hot, then it is taxable, unless it is coffee then it might not be. If an item is cold, then it probably is not taxable, unless it is carbonated, then it is.

Having fun, yet?

Overriding everything about take-out orders is whether or not a restaurant *qualifies* to not charge sales tax on take-out orders. That depends on what percentage of their customers dine-in as opposed to take-out. If too many dine-in, then the restaurant is required to charge sales tax on every order whether the customer is dining-in or taking-out.

Even if a restaurant does qualify to differentiate between dine-in and take-out orders, many choose not to deal with this complicated mess. They just charge everyone sales tax on everything. Which is perfectly okay with the CDTFA, so long as the CDTFA gets all the taxes.

Catering

In general, if you provide and serve food, then it is all subject to sales tax just like a restaurant's dine-in customers.

If you are not serving the food, but just delivering it, then just the hot food and carbonated beverages are taxable.

There are exceptions to this, of course. If you deliver a cake to a wedding, then that cake is not taxable – unless it is sliced (the CDTFA says sliced cake is taxable…???).

And, if you sell a cake and charge separately for the cake stand (whether as a sale or rental), then the charge for the cake stand is taxable, even if the cake is not. This would also apply to the rental of tables, chairs, decorations, etc. Tangible personal property is subject to sales tax if rented, just as it is when sold.

Real Estate

As I mentioned earlier, real estate is not taxable, and in general, anything attached to real estate is also not taxable.

For example, wallpaper is not taxable if you install it and the installation is included in your lump sum sales price. Of course, if you sell wallpaper without installing it, then it is taxable. If you sell the wallpaper and installation separately, then the wallpaper is taxable and the installation is not.

There are some things, however, that are taxable even though they are attached to real estate as part of the sale.

Equipment is taxable even if it is installed and permanently affixed to the real estate. That would include home theater equipment and security equipment.

Window coverings are taxable even if they are installed. That would include drapes and curtains. However, there is an exception to this exception; shutters are not taxable.

Carpet is not taxable if installed, but rugs are taxable because they are not affixed. Wood floors are not taxable, even when they are *floating* wood floors, meaning they are not permanently affixed.

The only sense I can make out of this is that the CDTFA must have some threshold regarding the meaning of the term *permanently affixed* as it applies to real estate. Perhaps they feel that if something is not *easily* removed, then it is permanent. Like shutters are harder to remove than curtains and floating wood floors are harder to remove than rugs.

Of course, I am guessing here. Who really knows what logic might lurk in the minds of the California politicians and special interest groups responsible for these rules?

Labor

Labor is generally not taxable.

However, if the labor is used to manufacture something that is taxable, then that labor is taxable. For example, if you sell someone all the materials needed to build a couch, those materials are taxable. If you also charge them to assemble the couch, then that assembly labor is also taxable.

The CDTFA looks at the entire transaction as the sale of a couch. They call the labor portion *fabrication labor* and require you to charge sales tax on it also.

There is another labor exception that I mentioned in Mistake #3, the handling portion of shipping and handling is not considered labor by the CDTFA and it is taxable.

Caveat

One final caveat about all these rules and exceptions, these are the current rules, as of this writing, for the State of

California only. They are subject to change at any time, and they may or may not apply to any other location outside of California.

Therefore, it is imperative that you familiarize yourself with the most recent published rules available. And if you are operating outside of California, investigate the rules that apply to those locations.

Chapter 6

Tracking Sales & Use Tax in QuickBooks

QuickBooks is designed to track sales taxes charged to your customers. If you set it up and use it correctly, it will help you charge the correct sales tax on each sale, and it can also help you track any use taxes you may owe or credits you may have on tax-paid purchases.

If you do not charge your customers sales tax, skip this section and go to **Tracking Only Use Tax** on page 48.

Sales Tax Charged to Customers

Big Picture: To calculate customer sales tax, your accounting software must know what taxable items you sell, which of your customers are taxable, and where you have nexus.

There are six steps in QuickBooks to correctly calculate and track the sales tax you need to charge your customers:
1. Activate QuickBooks' sales tax feature.
2. Set up sales tax items.
3. Assign every customer a sales tax item.
4. Flag items you sell that are taxable.
5. Use the Sales Tax Liability report to file your sales tax return.
6. Correctly enter your sales tax payments.

1. Activate QuickBooks' Sales Tax Feature

You might need to activate the Sales Tax feature in QuickBooks if it has not already been activated:

- Go to the Sales Tax Preferences screen by clicking on *Edit\ Preferences\ Sales Tax*.
- Then click on the *Company Preferences* tab.
- Click on *Yes* beside the question, *Do you charge sales tax?*

You will then be prompted to identify and set up your most common sales tax item. Follow the prompts and fill in the blanks. For example, you might set up OC Sales Tax with a Tax Rate of 7.75% and a Tax Agency of CDTFA (which you will then be prompted to set up as a vendor). When you are done, your sales tax item would look something like this:

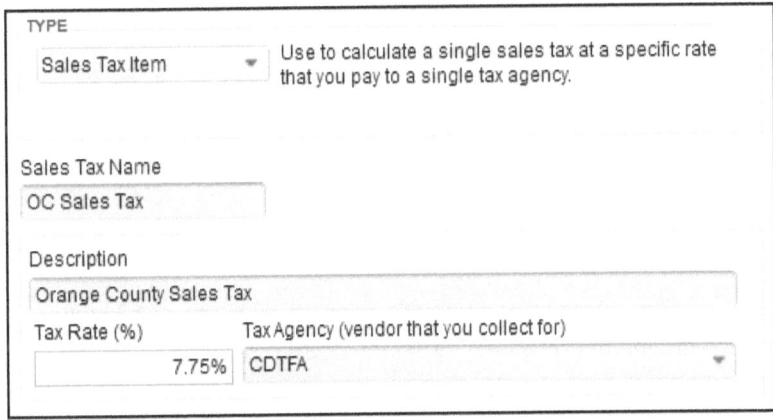

California only has one Sales Tax Agency. Some states have more than one and their setup is far more complex.

After you set up your Sales Tax Agency, QuickBooks will ask if you want to *Make all existing customers taxable* and/or if you want to *Make all existing non-inventory and inventory parts taxable*. I suggest you leave the check mark for *Make all existing customers taxable* (this will improve the information on your Sales Tax Liability report). Leave the other one checked if you have previously set up your taxable items as non-inventory parts or inventory parts. If not, then remove it. I will explain later how to select just those items that you want to flag as taxable.

When the Sales Tax feature is activated, QuickBooks sets up an Other Current Liability account called *Sales Tax Payable*. Any sales tax you charge your customers will automatically be posted to this account by QuickBooks.

2. Set Up Sales Tax Items

Now you are ready to set up a Sales Tax Item for every location where you have nexus.

From the Item List screen:
- Right click anywhere on the item list.
- Click *New*.
- Select *Sales Tax Item* as the *Type*.
- For each new item, fill in a *Sales Tax Name, Description, Rate,* and *Tax Agency* (like how you set up your most common sales tax item).

If you sell in just one location, you may only need your most common sales tax item. However, if you ship products to customers, you might need a sales tax item for California Sales Tax with the state's rate (as of this writing it is 7.25%).

You may also need other sales tax items like Reseller, Out-of-State, Fed Govt, or Indian Res all with tax rates of 0%. The reason for multiple sales tax items with 0% tax rates is because the CDTFA requires you to report any sales you make to Resellers, Out-of-State customers, the Federal Government, or Indian Reservations. By setting up these tax items and assigning them to your customers, all sales to them will be summarized on your Sales Tax Liability report.

3. Assign Sales Tax Items to Customers

Once you have set up all the Sales Tax Items you need, assign a sales tax item to each customer based on either their location or status (e.g. a Reseller's location does not matter).

From the Customer Center:
- Double click a customer to open *Edit Customer*.
- Click on the *Sales Tax Settings* tab.
- Leave the *Tax Code* as *Tax* or change it to *Tax* if it is *Non* (this improves the information on the Sales Tax Liability report).
- Select the appropriate *Tax Item* for this customer from the drop-down list.
- Enter the *Resale Number* for resale customers (be sure you have a resale certificate on file for each reseller as explained earlier in Mistake #4).
- Click *OK*.
- Repeat the above for every customer.

4. Flag Items You Sell that are Taxable

Your next step to correctly charging your customers sales tax is to flag every item you sell that is taxable.

From the Item List screen:
- Double click on a taxable item.
- Select *Tax* from the *Tax Code* drop-down list.
- Click *OK*.
- Repeat the above for each taxable item you sell.

At this point, you have completed all of the following:
- Activated the sales tax feature in QuickBooks.
- Set up sales tax items for every location you have nexus plus any 0% sales tax items you need.
- Assigned every customer a sales tax item.
- Assigned every taxable item a tax code of *Tax*.

Now, whenever you enter an invoice, QuickBooks will automatically calculate sales tax on taxable items based on the customer's sales tax rate and add it to the invoice total.

The sales tax from each invoice will be added to your Sales Tax Payable account, and you will be able to see how much you owe in sales tax at any time by simply looking at the balance in your Sales Tax Payable account.

5. Use the Sales Tax Liability Report

When you are ready to file your sales tax return, all the information you need regarding the sales tax you charged

Tracking Sales & Use Tax

your customers is listed on the Sales Tax Liability report. To run the report, click on ***Vendors/ Sales Tax/ Sales Tax Liability***. Be sure to run the report covering the same dates as the period of your sales tax return.

This report provides you with your total sales, non-taxable sales, locations where your sales were made, tax rates, and the tax you collected in each location.

If you have set up QuickBooks correctly and you filled out your sales tax return correctly, then the amount you owe should be within a few dollars of the total of the Sales Tax Payable column on this report. It never matches exactly because the CDTFA requires you to round all the numbers you report to the nearest dollar.

If the total you owe is not within a few dollars of the Sales Tax Liability report, then something is wrong. Troubleshoot the return for errors first. If the return is correct, then look for data entry and/or setup errors in QuickBooks.

6. Entering Sales Tax Payments into QuickBooks

After filing your sales tax return, enter your sales tax payment into QuickBooks correctly. Otherwise, the Sales Tax Liability report will be inaccurate the next time you run it.

To enter your sales tax payment in QuickBooks, click on ***Vendors/ Sales Tax/ Pay Sales Tax***.

This opens the Pay Sales Tax screen. Click off all the lines and then change your local sales tax line amount so your total ***AMT. PAID*** equals your sales tax payment. When you click ***OK***, QuickBooks will reduce your checking and Sales

Tax Payable accounts accordingly, thereby keeping your Sales Tax Liability report accurate.

Credits on Tax-Paid Purchases

Big Picture: If a vendor charges you sales tax on something you resell (prior to you using it in any way), you can deduct that sales tax from what you owe the CDTFA.

If you do not have tax-paid purchases in your business, then you can skip this section and go directly to **Use Tax** on page 37.

If you do have tax-paid purchases, there are four steps needed to keep track of them:
1. Add a Tax-paid Purchase Credits account to your Chart of Accounts.
2. Separate the sales tax on everything you purchase that you resell (without having used it beforehand).
3. Deduct the credits on your tax return.
4. Clear the tax-paid purchase credits in QuickBooks (when you enter your sales tax payment).

1. Add a Tax-paid Purchase Credits Account

QuickBooks automatically set up a Sales Tax Payable account to accumulate any sales taxes charged to customers. We will create another account for credits. I prefer to group both accounts together, that way all sales tax liability accounts are subtotaled on the Balance Sheet.

Tracking Sales & Use Tax 33

Here is how to group them together:
- Open your Chart of Accounts list.
- Right click the *Sales Tax Payable* account.
- Click *Edit Account*.
- Change the name to *Customer Sales Tax*. This will allow us to create a new Sales Tax Payable account with all the other sales tax liability accounts as subaccounts of it.
- Click *Save & Close*.
- Right click anywhere on the *Chart of Accounts*.
- Click *New*.
- From the *Other Account Types* drop-down list select *Other Current Liability*.
- Click *Continue*.
- Enter an *Account Name* of *Sales Tax Payable*.
- Click *Save & New*.
- Enter an *Account Name* of *Tax-paid Purchase Credits*.
- Click the check-box for *Subaccount of*.
- Select *Sales Tax Payable*.
- Click *Save & Close*.
- Right click on your newly renamed *Customer Sales Tax* account.
- Click *Edit Account*.
- Click the check-box for *Subaccount of*.
- Select *Sales Tax Payable*.
- Click *Save & Close*.

When you are done, this section of your Chart of Accounts should look something like this:

NAME	⚡	TYPE	BALANCE ...
◆ Sales Tax Payable		Other Current Liability	0.00
◆ Customer Sales Tax		Other Current Liability	0.00
◆ Tax-paid Purchase Credits		Other Current Liability	0.00

2. Separate Sales Tax on Tax-Paid Purchases

Regardless of which QuickBooks screen you use to enter a purchase (***Enter Bills***, ***Enter Credit Card Charges***, or ***Write Checks***), if you are expensing the cost of the item on the ***Expenses*** tab of the screen (as you might for job costing), then the sales tax portion should be separated onto its own line and applied to ***Tax-paid Purchase Credits***.

For example, let's say you bought a tool from Home Depot that you will be reselling to a client. The price of the tool was $137.15 and the sales tax was $10.63 for a total purchase of $147.78. You would separate it like this:

E*x*penses	$147.78	Ite*m*s	$0.00
ACCOUNT			AMOUNT
Cost of Goods Sold			137.15
Sales Tax Payable:Tax-paid Purchase Credits			10.63

However, if you are purchasing an inventory item on the ***Items*** tab, then the sales tax portion should still be entered on the *Expenses* tab and applied to *Tax-paid Purchase Credits*. It would look more like this:

Expenses	$10.63	Items	$137.15
ACCOUNT			AMOUNT
Sales Tax Payable:Tax-paid Purchase Credits			10.63

If you enter the purchase directly into a register (bank or credit card account), click on the *Split* button at the bottom of the register and separate the credit like this:

	TYPE	ACCOUNT	MEMO	
05/02/2...	Ref	Home Depot		147.78
	CC	-split-	Memo	
ACCOUNT			AMOUNT	MEMO
Cost of Goods Sold			137.15	
Sales Tax Payable:Tax-paid Purchase Credits			10.63	

These credits will be negative numbers in the Tax-Paid Purchase Credits account and will reduce your Sales Tax Payable total on your Balance Sheet. They will also be readily available when it is time to file your sales tax return.

Remember, you only separate sales tax on something that you bought and will be reselling *prior* to using it yourself. For example, if you buy a display case that you plan to sell after you use it at a trade show, do not separate the sales tax on the purchase. If you use it at all, you do not get a credit for the sales tax. Why? Because the State of California says so.

3. Apply the Credits to Your Sales Tax Return

There is a line item on sales tax returns entitled ***Tax-paid Purchases Resold Prior to Use***. It is in the deductions section of the return. Enter the total amount of the *purchases* you had, and that will reduce the amount of sales tax you owe.

To calculate the total amount of purchases, divide the total amount of credits by your local tax rate. For example, say you have $273.15 in credits during the quarter and your local tax rate is 7.75%. Your total purchases would be $3,524.52 ($273.15 divided by .0775), and you would enter $3,525 as your ***Tax-paid Purchases Resold Prior to Use***.

This reduces the total taxable sales on the return. You may need to reduce your local taxable sales by this amount in the district section to keep the return balanced.

4. Clear Tax-paid Purchase Credits in QuickBooks

To enter your sales tax payment in QuickBooks, click on ***Vendors/ Sales Tax/ Pay Sales Tax***. Before entering your payment, enter a sales tax adjustment by clicking on ***Adjust***.

This opens your ***Sales Tax Adjustment*** screen. Enter your ***Sales Tax Vendor*** as CDTFA, your ***Adjustment Account*** as Tax-paid Purchase Credits, and the adjustment amount as ***Reduce Sales Tax By***. If you date the adjustment for the end of the filing period, then the Tax-paid Purchase Credits account will start the new period at zero.

When you click ***OK***, the ***Pay Sales Tax*** screen will display the adjustment on a separate line. Click off all the lines and then change your local sales tax line amount so your total *AMT. PAID* equals your sales tax payment.

Use Tax

Big Picture: If you buy something to use in your business and your vendor does not charge you sales tax, you are required to pay use tax to the State of California.

There are four steps to help you keep track of use tax:
1. Add a Use Tax Payable account to your Chart of Accounts.
2. Add use tax to all taxable purchases without sales tax and book the use tax to Use Tax Payable.
3. Add the use tax owed to your sales tax return.
4. Clear the Use Tax Payable in QuickBooks (when you enter your sales tax payment).

1. Add a Use Tax Payable Account

If you set up a Tax-paid Purchase Credits account from the previous section, then skip down to **Add Just a Use Tax Payable Account** on page 39.

If you do not need and did not set up a Tax-paid Purchase Credits account from the previous section, then continue here.

QuickBooks has already set up a Sales Tax Payable account for you. Now we want to create another account for the use taxes you owe the CDTFA. My preference is to group them together, so all sales and use tax liability accounts are subtotaled on the Balance Sheet. Here is how:

- Open your Chart of Accounts list.
- Right click on the *Sales Tax Payable* account.
- Click *Edit Account*.
- Change the name to *Customer Sales Tax*. This will allow us to create a new Sales Tax Payable account with all the other sales tax liability accounts as subaccounts of it.
- Click *Save & Close*.
- Right click anywhere on the *Chart of Accounts*.
- Click *New*.
- From the *Other Account Types* drop-down list select *Other Current Liability*.
- Click *Continue*.
- Enter an *Account Name* of *Sales Tax Payable*.
- Click *Save & New*.
- Enter an *Account Name* of *Use Tax Payable*.
- Click the check box for *Subaccount of*.
- Select *Sales Tax Payable*.
- Click *Save & Close*.
- Right click on the newly renamed *Customer Sales Tax* account.
- Click *Edit Account*.
- Click the check box for *Subaccount of*.
- Select *Sales Tax Payable*.
- Click *Save & Close*.

Tracking Sales & Use Tax

When you are done, this section of your Chart of Accounts should look something like this:

NAME	TYPE	BALANCE
◇ Sales Tax Payable	Other Current Liability	0.00
◇ Customer Sales Tax	Other Current Liability	0.00
◇ Use Tax Payable	Other Current Liability	0.00

Since you just set up your Use Tax Payable account, skip down to **2. Add Use Tax to a Purchase** on the next page.

Add Just a Use Tax Payable Account

If you set up a Tax-Paid Purchase Credits account, then here is how to add a Use Tax Payable account to your Chart of Accounts so all of your sales and use tax liabilities will be subtotaled on your Balance Sheet:

- Open your Chart of Accounts list.
- Right click anywhere on the *Chart of Accounts*.
- Click *New*.
- From the *Other Account Types* drop-down list select *Other Current Liability*.
- Click *Continue*.
- Enter an *Account Name* of *Use Tax Payable*.
- Click the check box for *Subaccount of*.
- Select *Sales Tax Payable*.
- Click *Save & Close*.

When you are done, this section of your Chart of Accounts should now look something like this:

NAME		TYPE	BALANCE ...
◆ Sales Tax Payable		Other Current Liability	0.00
◆ Customer Sales Tax		Other Current Liability	0.00
◆ Tax-paid Purchase Credits		Other Current Liability	0.00
◆ Use Tax Payable		Other Current Liability	0.00

2. Add Use Tax to a Purchase

Regardless of which QuickBooks screen you use to enter a purchase (**Enter Bills**, **Enter Credit Card Charges**, or **Write Checks**), you probably use the **Expenses** tab of the screen to expense the cost. However, your actual cost should include sales tax even if your vendor failed to charge you for it.

Enter the amount you paid (or owe) the vendor in the total payment (or Amount Due) field at the top of the screen. Then add your local sales tax to the expense line amount. Only increase the expense, not the total.

To calculate your cost plus use tax, multiply the cost of the item (not including non-taxable delivery or fees) by 1 plus your local tax rate. Then add any non-taxable delivery or fees. The total is what your vendor should have charged you.

For example, let's say you paid $220 for office supplies and $15 for shipping from an out-of-state vendor. Your total payment was $235. If your local sales tax rate is 7.75%, then calculate the total cost of your office supplies by multiplying the $220 by 1.0775 (1 + 7.75%) and then adding the $15. Your total expense comes to $252.05 for the office supplies.

Enter $252.05 on the first expense line and book it to your Office Supplies expense account. When you drop down to the next expense line on the screen, QuickBooks will automatically enter a negative number (the difference between what you should have paid for the purchase and the amount you actually paid). This negative number is the amount of use tax that you just added to your expense. Book this negative number to your Use Tax Payable account.

In this example, the negative number would be $17.05 ($220 times 7.75%). This is the amount of use tax you owe the CDTFA on this purchase.

When you have entered this transaction correctly, the screen should look something like this:

Expenses $235.00	Items $0.00
ACCOUNT	AMOUNT
Office Supplies & Expenses	252.05
Sales Tax Payable:Use Tax Payable	-17.05

If you are entering a purchase on the *Items* tab, then you would still add the sales tax to the cost of the item and the negative use tax amount would be entered on the *Expenses* tab and applied to *Use Tax Payable*. Something like this:

Expenses -$17.05	Items $252.05
ACCOUNT	AMOUNT
Sales Tax Payable:Use Tax Payable	-17.05

If you enter the purchase directly into a register (bank or credit card account), click on the ***Split*** button at the bottom of the register and separate the use tax like this:

	TYPE	ACCOUNT	MEMO	
05/02/2...	Ref	HP Home Store		235.00
	CC	-split-	Memo	

ACCOUNT	AMOUNT	MEMO
Office Supplies & Expenses	252.05	
Sales Tax Payable:Use Tax Payable	-17.05	

Some vendors may charge you sales tax, but less than your local sales tax rate. For example, your local rate may be 7.75% and your vendor may charge you the California rate of 7.25%. Maybe they have nexus in California, but not in your district. You are still responsible for the difference.

Calculate what the total purchase should have been with the correct sales tax rate and book it as above.

Let's take our earlier example and say you paid $220 for office supplies and $15 for shipping from your vendor, and they also charged you sales tax of $15.95 (7.25% on the $220). Your total payment was $250.95.

If your local sales tax rate is 7.75%, then calculate the total cost of your office supplies by multiplying the $220 by 1.0775 (1 + 7.75%) and then adding the $15. Your total expense still comes to $252.05 for the office supplies.

In this case, the difference of $1.10 will be the negative amount you would book to Use Tax Payable like this:

Expenses	$250.95	Items	$0.00
ACCOUNT			AMOUNT
Office Supplies & Expenses			252.05
Sales Tax Payable:Use Tax Payable			-1.10

By entering purchases in this way, the use tax you owe will accumulate in the Use Tax Payable account and increase your overall Sales Tax Payable total on your Balance Sheet. It will also be readily available when it is time to file your sales tax return.

3. Add Use Tax to Your Sales Tax Return

There is a line on sales tax returns entitled ***Purchases Subject to Use Tax***. It is located under the ***Total Gross Sales*** line. When you enter the total amount of purchases on which you did not pay sales tax, the total amount owed on the return will increase by the amount of the use tax.

To calculate the total amount of purchases, simply divide the total amount of use tax by your local tax rate.

For example, if you have $273.15 in use tax during a quarter and your local tax rate is 7.75%, the total of your purchases would be $3,524.52 ($273.15 divided by .0775). Your ***Purchases Subject to Use Tax*** would be $3,525.

This increases the total taxable sales on the return. You may need to increase your local taxable sales by this amount in the district section of your return to keep it balanced.

4. Clear Use Tax Payable

To enter your sales tax payment in QuickBooks, click on ***Vendors/ Sales Tax/ Pay Sales Tax***. Before entering your payment, enter a sales tax adjustment by clicking on ***Adjust***.

This opens your ***Sales Tax Adjustment*** screen. Enter your ***Sales Tax Vendor*** as CDTFA, your ***Adjustment Account*** as Use Tax Payable, and the adjustment amount as ***Increase Sales Tax By***. If you date the adjustment for the end of the filing period, then the Use Tax Payable account will start the new period at zero.

When you click ***OK***, the ***Pay Sales Tax*** screen will display the adjustment on a separate line. Click off all the lines and then change your local sales tax line amount so your total ***AMT. PAID*** equals your sales tax payment.

Notes on Filing Sales Tax Returns

When you file your return, your total payment should be within a few dollars of the Sales Tax Payable total on your Balance Sheet at the end of the filing period.

For example, if you are filing your third quarter return, run your Balance Sheet with the date range set from 7/1 to 9/30. The total Sales Tax Payable will include all the sales taxes you charged customers, minus any credits you have for tax-paid purchases you resold prior to use, plus any use tax you owe because vendors did not charge you sales tax, and minus any monthly prepayments you have paid.

When preparing to file a quarterly sales tax return, I suggest you print the following reports with the *Dates* field set to the period covering your sales tax return:

- **Balance Sheet** – the total of Sales Tax Payable on this report is the amount you should be paying the CDTFA (within a few dollars).
- **Sales Tax Liability** - this report summarizes the customer sales and the sales tax collected. The *Sales Tax Payable* column should equal the total amount in *Customer Sales Tax* on your Balance Sheet. Aside from minor rounding, the only difference between the *Tax Collected* column and the *Sales Tax Payable* column on this report would be the total of any monthly prepayments made during the quarter.
- **Tax-paid Purchase Credits Detail** – double click the total *Tax-paid Purchase Credits* on the Balance Sheet. QuickBooks will list the transactions in that account for the period. Be sure to review these transactions for possible mistakes. You do not want to take a credit for sales tax you paid on something you used.
- **Use Tax Payable Detail** – double click the total *Use Tax Payable* on the Balance Sheet. QuickBooks will list the transactions in that

account for the period. Be sure to review these transactions also for possible mistakes.

If you have followed the setup and data entry instructions provided in this book, these four reports should provide you will all the numbers you need to file your sales tax return (although you will need to divide the amount of Tax-paid Purchase Credits and Use Tax Payable by your local sales tax rate as described earlier). And if you input these numbers correctly into your sales tax return, then the amount you owe should be within a few dollars of the total of your Sales Tax Payable accounts.

Keep in mind, it never matches exactly due to rounding. So, do not worry about being off a few bucks. However, if you are off by more than that, double check the return for any errors. If the return is correct, then double check your data entry and setup in QuickBooks until you get the amount due closer before you submit your return.

After you finish filing your sales tax return, I recommend you print it and staple it together with these four reports. In the event of an audit, the CDTFA will be able to see the logic behind the numbers you reported. Also, if any transactions get entered or edited later that might affect your return, these reports can help you locate those transactions.

Before you post your sales tax payment in QuickBooks, enter sales tax adjustments to zero out your Tax-paid Purchase Credits and Use Tax Payable accounts as described earlier. The adjustment for Tax-paid Purchase Credits would be a decreasing adjustment, and the adjustment for Use Tax Payable would be an increasing adjustment. Date the adjustments on the last day of the filing period and these two accounts will start the new period at zero.

Finally, after filing your sales tax return and posting the sales tax payment, advance your closing date in QuickBooks. You do not want anyone accidentally changing anything that might affect the sales tax return you just filed.

You can skip the next chapter. You already know how to track your use tax.

Chapter 7

Tracking Only Use Tax

Big Picture: If you buy something to use in your business and your vendor does not charge you sales tax, you are required to pay use tax to the State of California.

There are three steps to help you keep track of use tax:
1. Add a Use Tax Payable account to your Chart of Accounts.
2. Add use tax to all taxable purchases without sales tax and book the use tax to Use Tax Payable.
3. Enter your use tax payments into QuickBooks.

1. Add a Use Tax Payable Account

If you do not charge sales tax, then you do not need any Sales Tax Payable accounts. You only need a Use Tax Payable account. Here is how to set one up:
- Open your Chart of Accounts list.
- Right click anywhere on the *Chart of Accounts*.
- Click *New*.
- From the *Other Account Types* drop-down list select *Other Current Liability*.
- Click *Continue*.
- Enter an *Account Name* of *Use Tax Payable*.
- Click *Save & Close*.

2. Add Use Tax to a Purchase

Regardless which QuickBooks screen you use to enter a purchase (***Enter Bills***, ***Enter Credit Card Charges***, or ***Write Checks***), costs are typically entered on the ***Expenses*** tab. The cost should include sales tax even if your vendor did not charge you for it. So, enter the amount you paid (or owe) in the Total Payment (or Amount Due) field at the top of the screen. Then add your local sales tax to the expense line amount. Only increase the expense, not the total.

To calculate your cost plus use tax, multiply the cost of the item (not including non-taxable delivery or fees) by 1 plus your local tax rate. Then add any non-taxable delivery or fees. The total is what your vendor should have charged you.

Let's say you paid $220 for office supplies and $15 for shipping and your total payment was $235. If your local sales tax rate is 7.75%, then calculate the total cost of your office supplies by multiplying the $220 by 1.0775 (1 + 7.75%) and then adding the $15. Your total expense comes to $252.05 for the office supplies. Enter $252.05 on the first expense line and book it to your Office Supplies expense account.

Drop down to the next line, and QuickBooks automatically enters a negative number (the difference between what you should have paid for the purchase and the amount you actually paid). This negative number is the amount of use tax that you just added to your expense. Book this negative number to your Use Tax Payable account. In this example, the negative number would be $17.05 ($220 times 7.75%). This is the amount of use tax you owe on this purchase. When you have entered this transaction correctly, the screen should look something like this:

Expenses	$235.00	Items	$0.00
ACCOUNT			AMOUNT
Office Supplies & Expenses			252.05
Use Tax Payable			-17.05

If you enter the purchase on the *Items* tab, then you would still add the sales tax to the cost of the item and the negative use tax amount would be entered on the *Expenses* tab and applied to *Use Tax Payable*. Something like this:

Expenses	-$17.05	Items	$252.05
ACCOUNT			AMOUNT
Use Tax Payable			-17.05

If you enter the purchase directly into a register (bank or credit card account), click on the *Split* button at the bottom of the register and separate the use tax like this:

	TYPE	ACCOUNT	MEMO	
05/02/2...	Ref	HP Home Store		235.00
	CC	-split-	Memo	
ACCOUNT			AMOUNT	MEMO
Office Supplies & Expenses			252.05	
Use Tax Payable			-17.05	

Tracking Only Use Tax

Some vendors may charge you sales tax, but less than your local sales tax rate. For example, your local rate may be 7.75% and your vendor may charge you the California rate of 7.25%. Maybe they have nexus in California, but not in your district. You are still responsible for the difference.

Calculate what the total purchase should have been with the correct sales tax rate and book it as above.

Let's take our earlier example and say you paid $220 for office supplies and $15 for shipping from your vendor, and they also charged you sales tax of $15.95 (7.25% on the $220). Your total payment was $250.95. If your local sales tax rate is 7.75%, then calculate the total cost of your office supplies by multiplying the $220 by 1.0775 (1 + 7.75%) and then adding the $15. Your total expense still comes to $252.05 for the office supplies.

In this case, the difference of $1.10 will be the negative amount you would book to Use Tax Payable like this:

Expenses	$250.95	Items	$0.00
ACCOUNT			AMOUNT
Office Supplies & Expenses			252.05
Use Tax Payable			-1.10

By entering purchases in this way, the use tax you owe will accumulate in the Use Tax Payable account on your Balance Sheet. It will also be readily available when it is time to pay your use taxes.

3. Paying Use Taxes

You can pay use taxes by adding them to your California income tax return or filing a separate use tax return. Regardless of your filing method, the total amount you pay should be within a few dollars of the Use Tax Payable amount showing on your Balance Sheet at the end of the filing period.

For example, if you are paying your third quarter use taxes, run your Balance Sheet with the date range set from 7/1 to 9/30. Double click the amount of *Use Tax Payable* on the Balance Sheet, and QuickBooks will list all the transactions in that account for the quarter. Be sure to review these transactions for any possible mistakes.

If you follow these setup and data entry instructions, this report should provide you with the numbers you need to calculate your purchases subject to use tax.

To calculate the total amount of your purchases subject to use tax, simply divide the total amount of use tax by your local tax rate. For example, let's say you have $273.15 in use tax during the quarter. If your local tax rate is 7.75%, then the total of your purchases would be $3,524.52 ($273.15 divided by .0775), and you would enter $3,525 as your *Purchases Subject to Use Tax*.

After filing and paying your use taxes, print the return and staple it together with your report and calculations. In the event of an audit, the CDTFA will be able to see the logic behind the numbers you reported. Also, if any transactions get entered or edited later that might have affected your payment, these reports can help you locate those transactions.

To record the payment in QuickBooks, I suggest you enter a bill dated the end of the quarter for the amount of your use taxes. This will clear the Use Tax Payable account and transfer the amount to Accounts Payable. Then, enter a Bill Payment Check in QuickBooks and date it with the date you paid your use taxes.

Finally, after paying your use taxes and posting the use tax payment, advance your closing date in QuickBooks. You do not want anyone accidentally changing anything in that quarter that might affect the use tax taxes you just paid.

Contact Information

I hope you have found this information helpful. If you have any questions, please email me at:

Tim@ShortridgeBusinessServices.com

Acknowledgements

This book would not have been possible without the support and assistance of my wife, and best friend, Corky Shortridge. She also happens to be my editor, proof-reader, and best critic. Thank you, thank you, thank you.

Other Books by
Tim Shortridge

Non-fiction

UNDERSTAND ACCOUNTING Without Falling Asleep
  – Accounting Primer

Learn the basics in just 47 pages. When humor meets accounting, understanding wins. So, have a little fun while you learn.

In 1992, I started my own business setting up accounting systems for small businesses and teaching the owners how to use them. Over the years, I developed this simple explanation of accounting basics that has proven effective with my non-accountant clients. Not only do they understand basic accounting, but they also stay awake during the learning process. – Tim Shortridge

DON'T COOK FISH IN THE COMPANY MICROWAVE
– Career Advice

Do you look forward to going to work? If not, this book could help.

With a dash of humor, this book describes five simple steps to doing well and feeling good at work. It also includes 335 secrets and tips to help you advance your career (and which might just improve your life).

If your career is going great, but you are worried about how your children are doing at work, then this book would be a perfect gift for them. If your employees are not performing up to your standards, you should make this book required reading.

I have stumbled in my career so many times that it is embarrassing. Each time, it cost me dearly, either in time, money, or both. Mostly both. I wrote this book for my children because I did not want them to duplicate the career mistakes I have made. I have made it available to your children (and your parents' children) in hopes that it helps them, too. – Tim Shortridge

NO PLACE TO RUN
– Holocaust Memoir

David and Sophie Goetzel moved from Germany to Warsaw, Poland in 1937 to escape the rising Nazi anti-Semitism at home. When the Germans invaded two years later, David vowed to keep his loved ones alive.

With dogged determination, the help of people he befriended along the way, and luck, he guided his wife and two-year-old daughter through the siege of Warsaw, imprisonment by the Gestapo, confinement in the Warsaw ghetto, going into hiding on the Aryan side of the city, eventual internment in Bergen-Belsen, and a terrifying train ride that led to liberation in 1945.

David, his wife, and his daughter all survived.

Michael Frounfelter and I wrote this true story about my friend David Gilbert in the style of a suspense / thriller. We have been told it reads as if John Grisham had written **The Diary of Anne Frank**, *but with a happy ending. – Tim Shortridge*

Fiction

SEALING FATE – Suspense Novel

There is an arsonist on the loose in San Diego County igniting wild fires in the dry, overgrown canyons whenever the Santa Ana winds blow. Doctor Vanessa Tornen lives with her mother and daughter in a house that overlooks one of those canyons.

When Doctor Tornen completes her OB/GYN residency and accepts a position at a women's center, she thinks she may have found a job that will allow her to begin paying down her massive student debt and finally start getting her personal life together. Then a group of pro-life fanatics decides to shut down the women's center by threatening the employees and their families.

Doctor Tornen's entire world could come crashing down around her, if it does not go up in flames first.

JAKE – Children's Bedtime Story

Small dog. Big personality. With 22 full-color pages of humorous pictures and doggie monologue, JAKE is a great bedtime story book. It also makes a perfect gift for any beginning reader.

OUT OF PLUMB – Humorous Poems and Short Stories

Need a quick laugh? This humorous collection of quirkiness will have you chuckling in no time.

www.ingramcontent.com/pod-product-compliance
Lightning Source LLC
Chambersburg PA
CBHW031542210526
45464CB00003B/1114